TEA-CUP READING AND THE ART OF FORTUNE-TELLING BY TEA-LEAVES

TEA-CUP READING
: : AND THE ART OF : :
FORTUNE-TELLING BY TEA-LEAVES

By A

Highland Seer

With An Introduction By

James Norwood Pratt

Privately Published For

John Harney & Sons, Ltd.
&
James Norwood Pratt Tea Luxuries

First Edition

CONTENTS

ILLUSTRATIONS

INTRODUCTION

by
James Norwood Pratt

Who hasn't heard of reading tea leaves? If you buy this book, you may have the good fortune to discover that it is no joke but an exercise of insight and intuition, not infrequently shading over into genuine psychic ability.

Here is the oldest book in English on the subject, most probably, just recently rediscovered by the distinguished tea merchant John Harney. It is based on an authentic tradition that goes back several centuries which has been preserved for us by our anonymous author, 'a Highland Seer.' With practice, I suppose accurate and reliable information from the tea leaf oracle is possible; at least sometimes it seems so to me. Besides,

Perhaps the best thing to be said for reading tea leaves is that it can be quite thoroughly frivolous from start to finish. No messy entrails to inspect, no lugubrious departed spirits to invoke, no supposed medium's palm to cross with green. These are serious procedures. In reading tea leaves, seriousness is optional and often out of place altogether. All one needs is a friend or two, tea, of course, and this book to leaf through in more ways than one.

If really keen to get to the instructions, you may skip ahead to 'The Tea-Leaf Oracle' at the end of this introduction. Divination—fortune-telling if you insist—is something I've thought about for a long time and there's a good deal I'd like to say before we return to the reading of tea leaves, which, in due course, we shall.

Highly Selective And Correspondingly Superficial Remarks on Divination

My first experience of fortune-telling was the Thanksgiving of my 20th year. An interest in anything vaguely occult had led me to invest in Tarot cards and a guide to their use by a turgid and pompous Victorian author named A.E. Waite. A fellow student was my first guinea pig. I laid out the cards just as the book directed and plodded through the arrangement, reading the meaning Mr. Waite attributed to each card. It was probably the most thoroughly amateurish performance of any occult ceremony in history. It was patently absurd to boot, for my friend faced the brightest of futures without a cloud on his horizon and the cards predicted nothing but difficulty and disappointment. The next time I ran into my subject a year had passed and I had forgotten the whole episode. Who could have guessed, he said, a little awestruck, his life had turned out exactly as the cards had foretold.

Over the years since then I have become somewhat familiar with seership, divination, oracles, prophecy, etc., which are often approved of by the same people who condemn 'fortune-telling'. I continued to play with the Tarot for about a decade, long enough to be able to dispense with guidebooks anyway. I gradually got into the I Ching. For a while I even owned a crystal ball, though I can't say I ever saw anything in it when sober. Over the years my fascination has compelled me to read a shelf of books more or less on the subject. I say more or less because the subject of divination is a broad one and covers a bewildering variety of practices in almost every culture from the most ancient times to the present.

Amongst the most impressive experiences of my life are a couple of predictions others made of my future which turned out to be spot on. A psychic once told me out of the blue that I was about to fall in love and damned if I didn't—madly, blindly, disastrously as it turned out, and only three months later. Not too long ago the proprietor of a cafe on an Aegean beach foretold an unimaginable treachery that lay in store for me and within four months this too had come to pass. This cafe proprietor was someone I met in Bodrum, Turkey, whose only contact with me came from reading my "fa'al"—Arabic (and Turkish) for fortune.

If you don't 'believe in' this sort of thing I invite you simply to close the book. I am only too well aware of the arguments that can be brought against it, but "I have no will to try proof-bringing," as the poet puts it. The whole idea of 'scientific proof' outside of laboratory conditions is ridiculous anyway, when you stop to think about it. You cannot, for example, 'prove' that you're not secretly a Satanic Space Sister or Brother from a galaxy far away. The great C.G. Jung wrote a famous foreword to the *I Ching* in which he suggests 'synchronicity' as a possible explanation for how predictions work. The sentence I like best in his remarkable essay is "The less one thinks about the theory of the *I Ching*, the more soundly one sleeps."

The forecasts I've mentioned in my own case are alike only in being completely accurate and absolutely inexplicable. One was done almost professionally, you might say, by a gifted psychic in a near-trance state. The other, equally valid, came from a man who could not pronounce my name and was reading my cup simply as a pastime for my amusement. There are merely the most vivid examples amongst a myriad I could cite. Like the Tarot reading I gave my fellow student at Chapel Hill, they seem to show that whether solemn or completely casual, fortune-telling may turn out to be on the money.

The Ancient World & Delphi

Divination seems to be as old as any human endeavor there is, and though it was sometimes taken lightly in antiquity, it was never meant so. Think of Cassandra warning against the Trojan horse. Every Roman schoolboy understood the moral of the story of the admiral so eager for battle he ignored the omen and ordered the sacred chickens thrown overboard when told they would not drink. "They're drinking now," he wisecracked, "let's fight." Of course he lost disastrously.

The ancients looked for omens everywhere. The Etruscans specialized in augury based on the flight of birds, a method of forecasting the Romans preserved well into the Christian era. They also borrowed the Etruscan practice of haruspicy or inspecting entrails, which enlightened opinion never wholly accepted. Dour old Cato said he would be surprised if entrails-inspectors didn't exchange knowing grins when passing one another on the street. The Roman augur and haruspex were paid public officials, but there was also an age-old array of popular practices used in personal fortune-telling, from astrology and dream interpretation to mediumship and the *sortes Vergilianae* or Virgilian lottery. You opened the *Aeneid* at random and put your finger on a line, which was the answer to your inquiry if only you managed to interpret it right. Christians later used the Bible in the same way, and Muslims the Koran.

The first Christian Roman Emperor, Constantine, erected in the circus or hippodrome of his new capital city a monumental pedestal of brass in the form of three coiled snakes which the Greeks had dedicated after their victory over the Persians at Platea in 479 BC. This ancient artifact, which stands in Istanbul to this day, formerly supported a gold tripod before the entrance to the temple at Delphi. (It remained intact until the early 1700s, when the heads of the serpents were broken off for some reason.) By the time the oracle of Delphi was finally closed in the name of Christianity in 390 AD, it had served as the center for divination in the ancient world for over a thousand years. We readers of tea leaves are successors, in a way, to the ancient Pythia who prophesied in Delphi's sacred precincts and it can do us no harm to consider, briefly, our antecedents.

Apollo's oracle was known throughout the Greek world by 700 BC and subsequent Greeks placed its foundation in the earliest days of the world. Modern archeologists can only assert that the site was in use a thousand years before the first stone temple was erected in the 700s BC; this temple was destroyed by fire circa 548 BC and its much larger replacement by earthquake in 373 BC. Then was built the temple whose remains are still to be seen today at Delphi, surely the most imposing setting in all of Greece. Delphi is situated about 2000 feet up the slopes of Mount Parnassus, poised between soaring, luminous rocks above and the olive-clad valley below. Nowhere is the effect of the rich, blue Mediterranean sky with its diaphanous light more remarkable. The ancients had other oracles but none with a more inspiring location.

A good deal is known about the oracular procedures, but much remains mysterious. The Pythia, as Apollo's priestess was called here, underwent a period of fasting and various rituals of purification before she would enter the inner sanctum of the temple. There she was given leaves of the laurel or bay, sacred to the god, to chew on while a small fire of laurel leaves and barley was ignited on the altar. Then, after a drink of holy water from a stream that flowed into the temple, she took her seat upon a tripod to deliver the oracle. In every account of a consultation we are told that the inquirers spoke directly to the Pythia (or the god) and that then the Pythla (or the god) responded directly to them. The responses were sometimes obscure and enigmatic, but other times they were straightforward and unequivocal, as when the oracle pronounced Socrates the wisest man alive. Or consider the oracle's last utterance, circa 360 AD, in reply to an inquiry from Julian, the last pagan Emperor:

> "Go tell the king: The carven hall is fallen in decay.
> Apollo has no chapel left, no prophesying bay,
> No talking spring. The stream is dry that had so much to say."

A modern misinterpretation of ancient sources is responsible for the widespread but mistaken belief that the Pythia inhaled intoxicating vapors from a cleft in the rock inside the sanctuary. We moderns also tend to overlook the fact that this sanctuary was reputed to contain the tomb of Dionysos, who ruled over Delphi for the three winter months. We tend to juxtapose Apollo, the god of clarity and consciousness, with the younger god of vegetation and the irrational, but an ancient would consider such dualism just as simple-minded as our idea that the 'spiritual' is pitted against the 'material.' In reality they are integrally related. Nature is a manifestation of divinity and, as Plato put it, time is a moving image of eternity. The esoteric dimension of Greek religious thought is rich with hints that illuminate the workings of divination.

A distinguished professor emeritus of classics at Berkeley, Joseph Fontenrose, has written a 500- page book entitled *The Delphic Oracle* in which he assembles all that is known on the subject and manages at the same time to miss the central point entirely. A superstitious lot our ancient ancestors may have been, but stupid they were not. An institution like Delphi could not have persisted in use for over a millennium—with its advice heeded, as it was—if its utterances did not prove of practical value to its inquirers. Today Delphi can be reconsidered in the light of what we have learned since 1959 about the workings of state and other oracles in Tibet.

The Modern World & Tibet

Before the Chinese takeover in 1959, the government of Tibet regularly consulted an oracle who was installed and maintained at a special monastery— Nechung—near Lhasa. As translations and first-hand accounts have proliferated over recent years, we have learned a good deal about these practices from sources as impeccable as the Dalai Lama and, interestingly, also from Lopsang Lhalungpa, the son of a former oracle. These oracles were male and generally short-lived, as the strain of undergoing possession by supernatural beings took a tremendous physical toll on their human channels. From time to time one would be dismissed for malfeasance of some sort, which shows the all-too-human temptation to abuse which must accompany sooth-saying at any time and place. All Tibetan oracles were supposed to be spiritually pure in order to exclude contact with evil forces. The particular supernatural being who possessed and spoke through the Nechung oracle was Dorje Drakden, also known as Tibet's Protector of Religion.

The ritual of consultation was elaborate. Sitting on his throne in the Nechung assembly hall, the oracle slowly went into a trance to the sound of deep chants and invocations by the Nechung monks. Only when he was deep in trance could he support the weight of his ritual headdress, which was so heavy it required two men to lift it onto his head. He then rose and danced beneath this weight, finally prostrating himself three times before the image of Tibet's great tantric mystic Padmasambhava and then before the Dalai Lama himself. A list of questions was then read to him by a high official and the oracle gave his answers, which were transcribed on the spot for the official government records. The Tibetan government-in-exile consults this oracle in modified form still today.

The medium, it might be noted, passes into unconsciousness immediately following possession and awakes with no memory of the event. Whereas the Pythia is described as speaking in her normal voice at Delphi, the

Nechung oracle speaks in an ethereal, halting hollow tone suggesting immense age and distance. A lengthy description of these procedures is to be found in John Avedon's biography of the Dalai Lama, along with abundant references to other oracles. In his autobiography the Dalai Lama himself gives further details and mentions the tender personal regard Dorje Drakden exhibits for him. As a state institution, Nechung monastery stood at the apex of a nationwide system consisting of thousands of mediums and their respective spirits, and this intercourse between human and non-human beings has been carried on uninterruptedly for some thirteen centuries.

Further Selective and Superficial Remarks

In Tibet and throughout Asia generally, not only oracles but a variety of methods of foretelling the future with varying degrees of sophistication and complexity continues to be employed and divination remains a normal and unquestioned part of life. With the evidence of accurate divination now available, even the most moronic materialists should find themselves obliged to admit, with Horatio, that there are indeed more things in heaven and earth than dreamt of in our philosophy. As for the thousand doubts, questions, and criticisms these strange powers may stir, I can answer these only by quoting once more Dr. C.G. Jung: "The irrational fullness of life has taught me never to discard anything, even when it goes against all our theories (so short-lived at best) or otherwise admits of no immediate explanation."

Let us leave the insoluble mystery of oracles and mediumship, which are not involved in most divination anyway. Among the doubts, questions, and criticisms possible, let us by all means avoid such heavy questions as whether life is fore-ordained and predestined or whether at least some freedom of choice is possible. Pondering the nature of time also gives me a headache, so I omit all mention of that issue. There are still a few considerations concerning foretelling the future with which to cudgel our brains. For instance:

Everything must mean something, or else nothing would mean anything. Think about this. Another way to phrase it might be: Everything that happens, no matter what, is an inconceivably improbable coincidence. Here you are—and no other person—reading this book—and no other book—just at this moment—and no other moment. How did this come about? Had the events of the last hour, even the last several minutes, gone ever so slightly different, you would not be reading this sentence just now. Now consider all the factors stretching back into all eternity which have contributed, each in its precise degree, to bringing you to this very place with this unlikely book in your hand. What a fantastic improb-ability! Yet here we are. Viewed in this light, every phenomena whatsoever is equally improbable—and infinitely so! There's nothing 'mere' about coincidence—the universe is *nothing but* coincidence.

We individuals are part of a seamless web, the continuous whole of reality. It seems to me that a person who is totally unsympathetic to fortune-telling has an unbalanced mind, trapped in the straightjacket of our time and cut off from the underlying patterns of existence which give life its meaning. You might imagine our 'reality' as a tube of time extending through space. We are constantly moving through this tube along with everything we perceive. Now if we could slice through the tube at a certain, perhaps perplexing, moment and study this cross-section, we would see down to the minutest, nonsensical detail the elements presently coinciding and the pattern formed by their immediate relationships to one another. Evaluating present patterns and relationships amongst disparate, apparently 'meaningless' things allows us to divine what to expect in the future. I believe this is why the most common method of seeking oracles involves the inspection of some sort of pattern—whether in the flight of birds, the fall of coins, as with the I Ching, or, yes, the leaves in the bottom of a teacup.

None of this makes the procedure or its outcome any less mysterious, of course but there you have it. Whatever happens at a given moment inevitably possesses the quality peculiar to that moment and no other. In my years as a professional wine critic and writer, I often saw colleagues judge correctly just from the appearance, taste and behavior of a wine the site of the vineyard and the year of its origin. A sister who deals in English antiques can with uncanny accuracy frequently name the time and place of origin and even the maker of a piece of furniture merely by looking at it. Several astrologers of my acquaintance can look at you and tell the position of the sun and moon and what sign of the Zodiac was rising above the horizon at the moment of your birth. I advance these facts as a purely practical argument that moments can leave long-lasting traces.

Now for the leap: We have to assume that these 'accidents' or 'coincidences' are in some way linked with the unconscious mind. The explanation for all prophecy and clairvoyance apart from mediumistic inspiration or possession boils down to the assumption that the unconscious already 'knows' the answer the question. There clearly are powers of exchange beyond the senses and the muscles, but the conscious mind has the thick skin of a rhinoceros; it is powerful but insensitive. It is what separates us from a sense of connection with the rest of the universe. We spend most of our lives trapped in this one area of the mind. As I sit here writing on a sunny morning looking out across San Francisco Bay, I am only 'theoretically' aware that I even have an unconscious mind. I cannot see it or feel it. It's like an arm I've been lying on in my sleep, which has become quite numb and feelingless. Strangely enough contemplating patterns of cards or coins or tea leaves can serve to restore circulation to these regions of the mind and gain us admittance to our hidden awareness.

The use of this perfectly normal power of the human soul involves entering a state of mind that is both purposeful and yet passive, relaxed. Mediums, psychics, and sensitives have developed this capacity to an extraordinary degree, no doubt, but all of us possess it. A little practice will most likely allow you to experience this for yourself. In *The Sixth Sense* (1927) Joseph Sinel described a friend who read tea leaves as invariably starting "with the usual rigamarole about meeting a tall, fair lady or handsome man," but his expression would then change as he began to exhibit clairvoyance, sometimes trivial, sometimes serious. As you'll see for yourself, there's a knack to it but it's nonetheless quite simple. You use the pattern formed as the take-off point for your imagination, in a way, liberating the mind to admit ESP.

The Tea Leaf Oracle

As predicted, we have now returned to our tea leaves. There are more powerful methods, quite apart from mediumship and oracles, which may produce profound, heavy duty results, but they require heavy duty commitment and disciplined training. Reading tea leaves is not the most powerful way to answer questions, look into the future, reveal the past or understand the present. But it too can produce accurate and startling results. You may not learn everything there is to know about reading tea leaves, but you can certainly learn enough to make it worth your while. All that's required is an open mind and a spirit of adventure, or even of light-hearted fun.

Reading tea leaves is fun, whether you become adept at it or not. It certainly doesn't hurt to number it among one's social attainments and the devious will find it especially useful in courting and other situations. The author of *Tom Jones* said scandal and gossip are the best sweeteners of tea, and nothing beats a peek at the future after one has finished it. Just be careful. As my own experience proves, you may speak more truly than you know. Further advice:

Assume there is an energy transfer or psychic rapport of some sort between the leaves in the cup and the individual consulting them. As our author says, "What matters is that the person shaking the dice, shuffling the dominoes, cutting the cards or turning the teacup, is by these very acts transferring from his mind where they lie hidden even from himself the shadows of coming events..." Some assert this allows the person to influence the arrangement of the leaves. The word parapsychologists have coined for this is psychokinesis. Others claim the importance of the inquirer's contact is that it allows the reader to practice 'psychometry,' which is what parapsychologists call discerning things from inanimate objects by clairvoyance.

Don't worry about how it works, just make sure the person for whom the reading is done prepares his or her own cup. Drinking the tea should provide contact enough, but to impregnate the leaves with one's energy for sure, it doesn't hurt to cover the cup with the hand for a minute or so. If asking a specific question, this is the time to concentrate on it. There are a number of points like these which our author omits, and a few others which could be amplified.

"It should be distinctly understood, however, that tea-cup fortunes are only horary, or dealing with two events of the hour or the succeeding twenty-four hours at furthest," we read. Not necessarily. Another experienced tea-leaf reader has shown me how to read a fortune for the next twelve months. The cup is read clockwise from the immediate left of the handle, which represents present time. Three months from now lies a quarter of the way around, six months directly across from the handle, nine months three-quarters around and a year hence at the immediate right of the handle. According to this scheme, symbols on the flat bottom of the cup pertain to the entire period. If a symbol lies partly on the bottom of the cup and partly on the side—say a four-leaf clover one-quarter of the way around—it should be interpreted as great good fortune beginning in about three months and continuing for the remainder of the year.

Remember that you must decide beforehand on the type of reading you want. A cup that is used to answer a question is valid only for that question. Expect the cup to foretell only the coming twenty-four hours unless you specifically inquire as to the next twelve months. In either case, nothing unimportant ever shows up in the cup and every symbol has significance, whether you can make it out at first or not.

"But how do I see these 'symbols'?" you may ask. The same way you see shapes and figures in clouds after gazing at them for a while. You don't have to force anything—take your time and the symbols sort of jump out at you. Take your time, turn the cup around this way and that, tilt it and examine the leaves from all angles. Contemplate quietly. If you rush, you won't see anything. It's not like watching television where the pictures just appear with no effort on your part. But when a symbol is there, it is just as clear as any form you see in a cloud. I should add that not all tea leaves give me a meaningful picture but remain merely blobs of wet leaf. When the cup contains little besides blobs of the sort, I take it to mean the day or year ahead contains nothing very noteworthy, which is also meaningful information of a sort.

A major consideration is the kind of tea you use and the way you prepare it. In theory this should not matter and certainly the Chinese, who use chiefly whole leaf teas, have always practiced tea-cup divination. Of this I know nothing; however, for purposes of using this book, teas of the type used by our author will no doubt give best results. It is clear from the illustrations that these were broken grade, small leaf teas—but not so fine as the dust our tea bags contain. I find the BOP and smaller grades of Indian and Ceylon teas available today work dandy. It's also okay to use a teaball or pot with a removable infuser basket provided you throw a half teaspoonful or more of tea directly into the pot. This way the cups will have leaves enough for fortune-telling left when the brew has been drunk.

About This Book

The identity of our author, 'a Highland Seer,' is unknown but I think it likely he or she was indeed Scottish, exactly as advertised. Amongst my other reasons for thinking so is the recurrence of the term 'spae-wife'—as obscure a bit of Scots dialect when this book was written, obviously during the First World War, as it is now. It derives from the Old Norse *spa* which means prophecy and was used by the Highlanders to denote those gifted with the 'second sight,' no great rarity among these rural Celtic clans folk even today.

The authenticity of any grimoire, book of spells, signs or the like rests upon the amount of tradition behind it, and I am inclined to accept the author's truthfulness in claiming: "Generations of spae-wives have found that the recurrence of a certain figure in the cup has corresponded with the occurrence of a certain event in the future lives of the various persons who have consulted them: and this empyrical (sic) knowledge has been handed down from seer to seer until a sufficient deposit of tradition has been formed from which it has been found possible to compile a detailed list of the most important symbols and to attach to each a traditional meaning. These significations have been collected by the writer—in a desultory manner—over a long period of years chiefly from sap-wives in both Highland and Lowland Scotland, but also in Cornwall, on Dartmoor, in Middle England, in Gloucetershire and Northumberland."

Any such dictionary of symbols must be taken as a starting point, of course, for the seer is describing landmarks on a voyage as they appeared to him or her and not as they would look on a map or from the air. There may be other ways to describe these things, but it must be said also that the symbols seem to have an existence strangely independent of the minds involved.

This is the oldest book on the subject I've ever come across and may well be the first such book published. Certainly 'Sepharial', 'Minetta' and a few other pseudonymous compilers since have pillaged it mercilessly. When John Harney discovered this book and asked me to write an introduction, we decided I should not edit or anywise alter the text. The present edition is a faithful replica of the work as written and seen through the press by 'a Highland Seer.'

PREFACE

It is somewhat curious that among the great number of books on occult science and all forms of divination which have been published in the English language there should be none dealing exclusively with the Tea-cup Reading and the Art of Telling Fortunes by the Tea-Leaves, notwithstanding that it is one of the most common forms of divination practiced by the peasants of Scotland and by village fortune-tellers in all parts of this country.

In many of the cheaper handbooks to Fortune-telling by Cards or in other ways only brief references to the Tea-cup method are given; but only too evidently by writers who are merely acquainted with it by hearsay and have not made a study of it for themselves.

This is probably because the Reading of the Tea-cups affords but little opportunity to the Seer of extracting money from credulous folk; a reason why it was never adopted by the gypsy soothsayers, who preferred the more obviously lucrative methods of "crossing the palm with gold or silver," or of charging a fee for manipulating a pack of playing-cards.

Reading the Cup is essentially a domestic form of Fortune-telling to be practiced at home, and with success by anyone who will take the trouble to master the simple rules laid down in these pages: and it is in the hope that it will provide a basis for much innocent and inexpensive amusement and recreation round the tea-table at home, as well as for a more serious study of an interesting subject, that this little guide-book to the science is confidently offered to the public.

TEA-CUP READING AND FORTUNE-TELLING BY TEA-LEAVES

CHAPTER I

INTRODUCTION TO THE ART OF DIVINATION FROM TEA-LEAVES

It seems highly probable that at no previous period of the world's history have there been so many persons as there are at the present moment anxious to ascertain in advance, if that be humanly possible, a knowledge of at least 'what a day may bring forth.' The incidence of the greatest of all wars, which has resulted in sparse news of those from whom they are separated, and produces a state of uncertainty as to what the future holds in store for each of the inhabitants of the British Empire, is, of course, responsible for this increase in a perfectly sane and natural curiosity; with its inevitable result, a desire to employ any form of divination in the hope that some light may haply be cast upon the darkness and obscurity of the future.

It is unfortunately the case, as records of the police-courts have recently shown, that the creation of this demand for fore knowledge of coming events or for information as to the well-being of distant relatives and friends has resulted in the abundant supply of the want by scores of pre tended 'Fortune-tellers' and diviners of the Future; who, trading upon the credulity and anxieties of their unfortunate fellow-countrywomen, seek to make a living at their expense.

Now it is an axiom, which centuries of experience have shown to be as sound as those of Euclid himself, that the moment the taint of money enters into the business of reading the Future the accuracy and credit of the Fortune told disappears. The Fortune-teller no longer possesses the singleness of mind or purpose necessary to a clear reading of the symbols he or she consults. The amount of the fee is the first consideration, and this alone is sufficient to obscure the mental vision and to bias the judgment. This applies to the very highest and most conscientious of Fortune-tellers—persons really adept at foreseeing the future when no taint of monetary reward intervenes. The greater number, however, of so-called Fortune-tellers are but charlatans, with the merest smattering of partly-assimilated knowledge of some form of divination or 'character-reading'; whether by the cards, coins, dice, dominoes, hands, crystal, or in any other pre tended way. With these, the taint of the money they hope to receive clouds such mind or intuition as they may possess, and it follows that their judgments and prognostications have precisely the same value as the nostrums of the quack medicine vendor. They are very different from the Highlander who, coming to the door of his cottage or bothie at dawn, regards steadfastly the signs and omens he notes in the appearance of the sky, the actions of animals, the flight of birds, and so forth, and derives therefrom a foresight into the coming events of the opening day. They differ also from the 'spae-wife', who, manipulating the cup from which she has taken her morning draught of tea, looks at the various forms and shapes the leaves and dregs have taken, and deduces thence such simple horary prognostications as the name of the person from whom 'postie' will presently bring up the glen a letter or a parcel or a remittance of money; or as to whether she is likely to go a journey, or to hear news from across the sea, or to obtain a good price for the hose she has knitted or for the chickens or eggs she is sending to the store-keeper. Here the taint of a money-payment is altogether absent; and no Highland 'spae-wife' or seer would dream of taking a fee for looking into the future on behalf of another person.

It follows, therefore, that provided he or she is equipped with the requisite knowledge and some skill and intuition, the persons most fitted to tell correctly their own fortune are themselves; because they cannot pay themselves for their own prognostications, and the absence of a monetary taint consequently leaves the judgement unbiased. Undoubtedly one of the simplest, most inexpensive and, as the experience of nearly three centuries has proved, most reliable forms of divination within its own proper limits, is that of reading fortunes in tea-cups although it cannot be of the greatest antiquity, seeing that tea was not introduced into Britain until the middle of the seventeenth century, and for many years thereafter was too rare and costly to be used by the great bulk of the population, the practice of reading the tea-leaves doubtless descends from the somewhat similar form of divination known to the Greeks as '*κοταβοζ*' by which fortune in love was discovered by the particular splash made by wine thrown out of a cup into a metal basin. A few spae-wives still practice this method by throwing out the tea-leaves into the saucer, but the reading of the symbols as they are originally formed in the cup is undoubtedly the better method.

Any person after a study of this book and by carefully following the principles here laid down may with practice quickly learn to read the horary fortunes that the tea-leaves foretell. It should be distinctly understood, however, that tea-cup fortunes are only horary, or dealing with the events of the hour or the succeeding twenty-four hours at furthest. The immediately forthcoming events are those which cast their shadows, so to speak, within the circle of the cup. In this way the tea-leaves may be consulted once a day, and many of the minor happenings of life foreseen with considerable accuracy, according to the skill in discerning the symbols and the intuition required to interpret them which may be possessed by the seer. Adepts like the Highland peasant-women can and do foretell events that subsequently occur, and that with remarkable accuracy. Practice and the acquirement of a knowledge of the signification of the various symbols is all that is necessary in order to become proficient and to tell one's fortune and that of one's friends with skill and judgment.

There is, of course, a scientific reason for all forms of divination practiced without hope or promise of reward. Each person carries in himself his own Destiny. Events do not happen to people by chance, but are invariably the result of some past cause for instance, in the last years a man becomes a soldier who had never intended to pursue a military career. This does not happen to him by chance, but because of the prior occurrence of a European war in which his country was engaged. The outbreak of war is similarly the result of other causes, none of which happened by chance, but were founded by still remoter occurrences. It is the same with the Future. That which a person does today as a result of something that happened in the past, will in its turn prove the cause of something that will happen at some future date. The mere act of doing something to day sets in motion forces that in process of time will inevitably bring about some entirely unforeseen event.

This event is not decreed by Fate or Providence, but by the person who by the committal of some act unconsciously compels the occurrence of some future event which he does not foresee. In other words, a man decrees his own destiny and shapes his own ends by his actions, whether Providence rough-hew them or not. Now this being so, it follows that he carries his destiny with him, and the more powerful his mind and intellect the more clearly is this seen to be the case. Therefore it is possible for a person's mind, formed as the result of past events over which he had no control, to foresee by an effort what will occur in the future as the result of acts deliberately done. Since it is given to but few, and that not often of intention, to see actually what is about to happen in a vision or by means of what is called the 'second sight', some machinery must be provided in the form of symbols from which an interpretation of the future can be made. It matters little what the method or nature of the symbols chosen is—dice or dominoes, cards or tea-leaves. What matters is that the person shaking the dice, shuffling the dominoes, cutting the cards or turning the tea-cup, is by these very acts transferring from his mind where they lie hidden even from himself the shadows of coming events which by his own actions in the past he has already predetermined shall occur in the future. It only remains for someone to read and interpret these symbols correctly in order to ascertain something of what is likely to happen; and it is here that singleness of purpose and freedom from ulterior motives are necessary in order to avoid error and to form a true and clear judgment.

This is the serious and scientific explanation of the little-understood and less-comprehended action of various forms of divination having for their object the throwing of a little light upon the occult. Of all these forms perhaps divination by tea-leaves is the simplest, truest, and most easily learned. Even if the student is inclined to attach much importance to what he sees in the cup, the reading of the tea leaves forms a sufficiently innocent and amusing recreation for the breakfast- or tea-table; and the man who finds a lucky sign such as an anchor or a tree in his cup, or the maiden who discovers a pair of heart-shaped groups of leaves in conjunction with a ring, will be suffering no harm in thus deriving encouragement for the future, even should they attach no importance to their occurrence, but merely treat them as an occasion for harmless mirth and badinage.

Whether, however, the tea-leaves be consulted seriously or in mere sport and love of amusement, the methods set forth in succeeding chapters should be carefully followed, and the significations of the pictures and symbols formed in the cup scrupulously accepted as correct, for reasons which are explained in a subsequent chapter.

CHAPTER II

RITUAL AND METHOD OF USING THE TEA-CUP

The best kind of tea to use if tea-cup reading is to be followed is undoubtedly China tea, the original tea imported into this country and still the best for all purposes. Indian tea and the cheaper mixtures contain so much dust and so many fragments of twigs and stems as often to be quite useless for the purposes of divination, as they will not combine to form pictures, or symbols clearly to be discerned.

The best shape of cup to employ is one with a wide opening at the top and a bottom not too small. Cups with almost perpendicular sides are very difficult to read, as the symbols cannot be seen properly ; and the same may be said of small cups. A plain-surfaced breakfast-cup is perhaps the best to use; and the interior should be white and have no pattern printed upon it, as this confuses the clearness of the picture presented by the leaves, as does any fluting or eccentricity of shape.

The ritual to be observed is very simple. The tea-drinker should drink the contents of his or her cup so as to leave only about half a teaspoonful of the beverage remaining . He should next take the cup by the handle in his left hand, rim upwards, and turn it three times from left to right in one fairly rapid swinging movement. He should then very slowly and carefully invert it over the saucer and leave it there for a minute, so as to permit of all moisture draining away.

If he approaches the oracle at all seriously he should during the whole of these proceedings concentrate his mind upon his future Destiny, and 'will' that the symbols forming under the guidance of his hand and arm (which in their turn are, of course, directed by his brain) shall correctly represent what is destined to happen to him in the future.

If, however, he or she is not in such deadly earnest, but merely indulging in a harmless pastime, such an effort of concentration not be made. The 'willing' is, of course, akin to 'wishing' when cutting the cards in another time-honoured form of fortune-telling.

The cup to be read should be held in the hand and turned about in order to read the symbols without disturbing them, which will not happen if the moisture has been properly drained away. The handle of the cup represents the consultant and is akin to the 'house' in divination by the cards. By this fixed point judgment is made as to events approaching the 'house' of the consultant, journeys away from home, messages or visitors to be expected, relative distance, and so forth. The advantage of employing a cup instead of a saucer is here apparent.

The bottom of the cup represents the remoter future foretold; the side events not be far distant; and matters symbolized near the rim those that may be expected to occur quickly. The nearer the symbols approach the handle in all three cases the nearer to fulfillment will be the events prognosticated.

If this simple ritual has been correctly carried out the tea-leaves, whether many or few, will be found distributed about the bottom and sides of the cup. The fortune may be equally well told whether there are many leaves or few; but of course there must be some, and therefore the tea should not have been made in a pot provided with one of the patent arrangements that stop the leaves from issuing from the spout when the beverage is poured into the cups. There is nothing to beat one of the plain old-fashioned earthenware teapots, whether for the purpose of preparing a palatable beverage or for that of providing the means of telling a fortune.

Chapter III

GENERAL PRINCIPLES TO BE OBSERVED IN READING THE CUP

The interior of the tea-cup when it is ready to be consulted will exhibit the leaves scattered apparently in a fortuitous and accidental manner, but really in accordance with the muscular action of the left arm as controlled by the mind at whose bidding it has worked. These scattered leaves will form lines and circles of dots or small leaves and dust combined with stems, and groups of leaves in larger or smaller patches: apparently in meaningless confusion.

Careful notice should now be taken of all the shapes and figures formed inside the cup. These should be viewed from different positions, so that their meaning becomes clear. It is not very easy at first to see what the shapes really are, but after looking at them carefully they become plainer. The different shapes and figures in the cup must be taken together in a general reading. Bad indications will be balanced by good ones; some good ones will be strengthened by others, and so on.

It is now the business of the seer— whether the consultant or some adept to whom he has handed the cup to be read— to find some fairly close resemblance between the groups formed by the leaves and various natural or artificial objects. This part of the performance resembles the looking for 'pictures in the fire' as practiced by children in nurseries and school rooms and occasionally by people of a larger growth. Actual representations of such things as trees, animals, birds, anchors, crowns, coffins, flowers, and so forth may by the exercise of the powers of observation and imagination be discerned, as well as squares, triangles, and crosses. Each of these possesses, as a symbol, some fortunate or unfortunate signification. Such signs may be either large or small, and their relative importance must be judged according to their size. Supposing the symbol observed should be that indicating the receipt of a legacy, for instance: if small it would mean that the inheritance would be but trifling, if large that it would be substantial, while if leaves grouped to form a resemblance to a coronet accompany the sign for a legacy, a title would probably descend upon the consultant at the same time. The meaning of all the symbols of this nature likely to be formed by the fortuitous arrangement of leaves in a tea-cup is fully set forth in the concluding chapter; and it is unnecessary therefore to enlarge upon this branch of the subject.

There are, however, several points of a more general character that must be considered before it is possible to form an accurate judgment of the fortune displayed. For instance, isolated leaves or groups of a few leaves or stems frequently form letters of the alphabet or numbers. These letters and numbers possess meanings which must be sought in conjunction with other signs. If near a letter L is seen a small square or oblong leaf, or if a number of very small dots form such a square or oblong, it indicates that a letter or parcel will be received from somebody whose surname (not Christian name) begins with an L. If the combined symbol appears near the handle and near the rim of the cup, the letter is close at hand; if in the bottom there will be delay in its receipt. If the sign of a letter is accompanied by the appearance of a bird flying towards the 'house' it means a telegraphic despatch: if flying away from the house the consultant will have to send the telegram. Birds flying always indicate news of some sort.

Again, the dust in the tea and the smaller leaves and stems frequently form lines of dots. These are significant of a journey, and their extent and direction shows its length and the point of the compass towards which it will extend: the handle for this purpose being considered as due south. If the consultant is at home and lines lead from the handle right round the cup and back to the handle, it shows that he will return; if they end before getting back to the handle, and especially if a resemblance to a house appears where the journey line ends, it betokens removal to some other place. If the consultant be away from home, lines leading to the handle show a return home, and if free from crosses or other symbols of delay that the return will be speedy: otherwise it will be postponed . The occurrence of a numeral may indicate the number of days, or if in connection with a number of small dots grouped around the sign of a letter, a present or a legacy, the amount of the remittance in the former, the number of presents to be expected, or the amount of the legacy coming. Dots surrounding a symbol always indicate money coming in some form or other, according to the nature of the symbol.

It will be seen that to read a fortune in the tea-cup with any real approach to accuracy and a serious attempt to derive a genuine forecast from the cup the seer must not be in a hurry. He or she must not only study the general appearance of the horoscope displayed before him, and decide upon the resemblance of the groups of leaves to natural or artificial objects, each of which possesses a separate significance, but must also balance the bad and good, the lucky and unlucky symbols, and strike an average. For instance, a large bouquet of flowers, which is a fortunate sign, would outweigh in importance one or two minute crosses, which in this case would merely signify some small delay in the realization of success; whereas one large cross in a prominent position would be a warning of disaster that would be little, if at all, mitigated by the presence of small isolated flowers, however lucky individually these may be. This is on the same principle as that by which astrologers judge a horoscope, when, after computing the aspects of the planets towards each other, the Sun and Moon, the ascendant, mid-heaven, and the significator of the

Native, they balance the good aspects against the bad, the strong against the weak, the Benefics against the Malefics, and so strike an average. In a similar way the lucky and unlucky signs in a tea-cup must be balanced one against the other and an average struck: and in this connection it may be pointed out that symbols which stand out clearly and distinctly by themselves are of more importance than those with difficulty to be discerned amid cloudlike masses of shapeless leaves. When these clouds obscure or surround a lucky sign they weaken its force, and vice versa.

In tea-cup reading, however, the fortune told must be regarded chiefly as of a horary character, not, as with an astrological horoscope, that of a whole life; and where it is merely indulged in as a light amusement to while away a few minutes after a meal such nicety of judgment is not called for. The seer will just glance at the cup, note the sign for a letter from someone, or that for a journey to the seaside or the proximity of a gift, or an offer of marriage, and pass on to another cup.

It should be observed that some cups when examined will present no features of interest, or will be so clouded and muddled that no clear meaning is to be read in them. In such a case the seer should waste no time over them. Either the consultant has not concentrated his or her attention upon the business in hand when turning the cup, or his destiny is so obscured by the indecision of his mind or the vagueness of his ideas that it is unable to manifest itself by symbols. Persons who consult the tea-leaves too frequently often find this muddled state of things to supervene. Probably once a week will be often enough to look into the future, although there is something to be said for the Highland custom of examining the leaves of the morning cup of tea in order to obtain some insight into the events the day may be expected to bring forth. To 'look in the cup' three or four times a day, as some silly folk do, is simply to ask for contradictory manifestations and consequent bewilderment, and is symptomatic of the idle, empty, bemused minds that prompt to such ill-advised conduct.

Of course the tea-cup may be employed solely for the purpose of asking what is known to astrologers as 'a horary question', such, for instance, as "Shall I hear from my lover in France, and when?" In this case the attention of the consultant when turning the cup must be concentrated solely on this single point, and the seer will regard the shapes taken by the tea-leaves only in this connection in order to give a definite and satisfactory answer. An example of this class of horary question is included among the illustrations (Fig. 10).

CHAPTER IV

AN ALPHABETICAL LIST OF SYMBOLS WITH THEIR SIGNIFICATIONS

A question that will very naturally occur to persons of an enquiring turn of mind in regard to the figures and symbols seen in the tea-cup is: Why should one symbol necessarily signify one thing and not something quite different.

The answer, of course, is that the meanings given to the symbols are purely arbitrary, and that there is no scientific reason why one should signify one thing and not another. There is no real reason why the ace of clubs, for instance, should not be considered the 'House Card' instead of the nine of hearts, or why the double four in dominoes should signify an invitation instead of a wedding, like the double three.

It is obviously necessary, however, in attempting to read the future by means of any kind of symbols, whether pips, dots, numbers or anything else, to fix beforehand upon some definite meaning to be attributed to each separate symbol and to hold fast to this meaning in all events. In the case of tea-leaves, where the symbols are not mere 'conventional signs' or numbers but actual figures like the pictures seen in the fire or those envisaged in dreams, there is no doubt that the signification of most of them is the result of empirical experience. Generations of spae-wives have found that the recurrence of a certain figure in the cup has corresponded with the occurrence of a certain event in the future lives of the various persons who have consulted them: and this empirical knowledge has been handed down from seer to seer until a sufficient deposit of tradition has been formed from which it has been found possible to compile a detailed list of the most important symbols and to attach to each a traditional meaning. These significations have been collected by the writer—in a desultory manner—over a long period of years chiefly from spae-wives in both Highland and Lowland Scotland, but also in Cornwall, on Dartmoor, in Middle England, in Gloucestershire and Northumberland. Occasionally it has been found that a different meaning is attributed to a symbol by one seer from that given it by another. In such cases an alternative signification might, of course, have been given here, but as the essence of all such significations is that they shall be stable and unvarying, the writer has fixed upon whichever meaning has been most widely attributed to the symbol or appears to have the best authority for its adoption, so that the element of doubt may be excluded.

Although included in their alphabetical order in the list which follows, there are certain figures and symbols which are of common occurrence and bear such definite interpretation that it is advisable to refer to them here in detail. Certain symbols are invariably signs of approaching good fortune: certain others of threatened ill-luck. Among the former may be mentioned triangles, stars, trefoil or clover-leaves, anchors, trees, garlands and flowers, bridges or arches, and crowns. Among the latter, coins, clouds, crosses, serpents, rats and mice and some wild beasts, hour-glasses, umbrellas, church steeples, swords and guns, ravens, owls, and monkeys are all ominous symbols.

Symbols and Significations

Abbey, future ease and freedom from worry.

Acorn, improvement in health, continued health, strength, and good fortune.

Aircraft, unsuccessful projects.

Anchor, a lucky sign; success in business and constancy in love; if cloudy, the reverse must be read.

Angel, good news, especially good fortune in love.

Apes, secret enemies.

Apples, long life; gain by commerce.

Apple-tree, change for the better.

Arch, a journey abroad.

Arrow, a disagreeable letter from the direction in which it comes.

Ass, misfortune overcome by patience; or a legacy.

Axe, difficulties overcome.

Badger, long life and prosperity as a bachelor.

Basket, an addition to the family.

Bat, fruitless journeys or tasks.

Bear, a long period of travel.

Beasts, other than those mentioned, foretell misfortune.

Birds, a lucky sign; good news if flying, if at rest a fortunate journey.

Boat, a friend will visit the consultant.

Bouquet, one of the luckiest of symbols; staunch friends, success, a happy marriage.

Bridge, a favorable journey.

Building, a removal.

Bull, slander by some enemy.

Bush, an invitation into society.

Butterfly, success and pleasure.

Camel, a burden to be patiently borne.

Cannon, good fortune.

Car (motor), and **Carriage**, approaching wealth, visits from friends.

Cart, fluctuations of fortune.

Castle, unexpected fortune or a legacy.

Cat, difficulties caused by treachery.

Cathedral, great prosperity.

Cattle, prosperity.

Chain, an early marriage; if broken, trouble in store.

Chair, an addition to the family.

Church, a legacy.

Circles, money or presents. They mean that the person whose fortune is read may expect money or presents.

Clouds, serious trouble; if surrounded by dots, financial success.

Clover, a very lucky sign; happiness and prosperity. At the top of the cup, it will come quickly. As it nears the bottom, it will mean more or less distant.

Cock, much prosperity.

Coffin, long sickness or sign of death of a near relation or great friend.

Comet, misfortune and trouble.

Compasses, a sign of traveling as a profession.

Cow, a prosperous sign.

Cross, a sign of trouble and delay or even death.

Crown, success and honor.

Crown and Cross, signifies good fortune resulting from death.

Dagger, favors from friends.

Deer, quarrels, disputes; failure in trade.

Dog, a favorable sign; faithful friends, if at top of cup; in middle of cup, they are untrustworthy; at the bottom means secret enemies.

Donkey, a legacy long awaited.

Dove, a lucky symbol; progress in prosperity and affection.

Dragon, great and sudden changes.

Duck, increase of wealth by trade.

Eagle, honour and riches through change of residence.

Elephant, a lucky sign; good health

Falcon, a persistent enemy.

Ferret, active enemies.

Fish, good news from abroad; if surrounded by dots, emigration.

Flag, danger from wounds inflicted by an enemy.

Fleur-de-lys, same as **Lily** (q.v.).

Flowers, good fortune, success; a happy marriage.

Fox, treachery by a trusted friend.

Frog, success in love and commerce.

Gallows a sign of good luck.

Goat, a sign of enemies, and of misfortune to a sailor.

Goose, happiness; a successful venture.

Grasshopper, a great friend will become a soldicr.

Greyhound a good fortune by strenuous exertion.

GUN, a sign of discord and slander.

HAMMER, triumph over adversity.

HAND, to be read in conjunction with neighbouring symbols and according to what it points.

HARE, a sign of a long journey, or the return of an absent friend. also of a speedy and fortunate marriage to those who are single.

HARP, marriage, success in love.

HAT success in life.

HAWK, an enemy.

HEART, pleasures to come; if surrounded by dots, through money; if accompanied by a ring, through marriage.

HEAVENLY BODIES, SUN, MOON, AND STARS, signifies happiness and success.

HEN, increase of riches or an addition to the family.

HORSE, desires fulfilled through a prosperous Journey.

HORSE-SHOE, a lucky journey or success in marriage and choosing a partner.

HOUR-GLASS, imminent peril.

HOUSE, success in business.

HUMAN FIGURES must be judged according to

what they appear to be doing. They are generally good and denote love and marriage.

INTERROGATION (mark of), doubt or disappoint.

IVY, honour and happiness through faithful friends.

JACKAL, a sly animal who need not be feared. A mischief maker of no account.

JOCKEY, successful speculation.

JUG, good health.

KANGAROO, a rival in business or love.

KETTLE, death.

KEY, money, increasing trade, and a good husband or wife.

KITE, a sign of lengthy voyaging and travel leading to honour and dignity.

KNIFE, a warning of disaster through quarrels and enmity.

LADDER, a sign of travel.

LEOPARD, a sign of emigration with subsequent success.

LETTERS, shown by square or oblong tea leaves, signifies news. Initials near will show surnames of writers; if accompanied by dots they will contain money; if unclouded, good; but if fixed about by clouds, bad news or loss of money.

LILY, at top of cup, health and happiness; a virtuous wife; at bottom, anger and strife.

LINES indicate journeys and their direction, read in conjunction with other signs of travel; wavy lines denote troublesome journeys or losses therein.

LION, greatness through powerful friends.

LYNX, danger of divorce or break off of an engagement.

MAN, a visitor arriving. If the arm is held out, he brings a present. If figure is very clear, he is dark; if indistinct, he is of light complexion.

MERMAID, misfortune, especially to seafaring persons.

MITRE, a sign of honour to a clergyman or through religious agency.

MONKEY, the consultant will be deceived in love.

MOON (as a crescent), prosperity and fortune.

MOUNTAIN, powerful friends; many mountains, equally powerful enemies.

MOUSE, danger of poverty through theft or swindling.

Mushroom, sudden separation of lovers after a quarrel.

Nosegay, the same as **Bouquet** (q.v.).

Numbers depends on symbols in conjunction with them. Or, very lucky; long life, good health, profitable business, and a happy marriage.

Oblong Figures, family or business squabbles.

Owl, an evil omen, indicative of sickness, poverty, disgrace, a warning against commencing any new enterprise. If the consultant be in love he or she will be deceived.

Palm-tree, good luck; success in any undertaking. A sign of children to a wife and of a speedy marriage to a maid.

Parrot, a sign of emigration for a lengthy period.

Peacock, denotes success and the acquisition of property; also a happy marriage.

Pear, great wealth and improved social position; success in business, and to a woman a wealthy husband.

Pedestrian, good news; an important appointment.

Pheasant, a legacy.

Pig, good and bad luck mixed: a faithful lover but envious friends.

Pigeons, important news if flying; if at rest, domestic bliss and wealth acquired in trade.

Pine-tree, continuous happiness.

Pistol, disaster.

Rabbit, fair success in a city or large town.

Rat, treacherous servants; losses through enemies.

Raven, death for the aged; disappointment in love, divorce, failure in business, and trouble generally.

Razor, lovers' quarrels and separation.

Reptile, quarrels.

Rider, good news from overseas regarding financial prospects.

Rifle, a sign of discord and strife.

Ring, a ring means marriage; and if a letter can be found near it, this is the initial of the future spouse. If clouds are near the ring, an unhappy marriage; if all is clear about it, the contrary. A ring right at the bottom means the wedding will not take place.

Rose, a lucky sign betokening good fortune and happiness.

Saw, trouble brought about by strangers.

Scales, a lawsuit.

Sceptre, a sign of honour from royalty.

Scissors, quarrels; illness; separation of lovers.

Serpents, spiteful enemies; bad luck; illness.

Shark, danger of death.

Sheep, success, prosperity.

Ship, a successful journey.

Snakes are a sign of bad omen. Great caution is needed to ward off misfortune.

Spider, a sign of money coming to the consultant.

Squares, comfort and peace.

Star, a lucky sign; if surrounded by dots foretells great wealth and honours.

Steeple, bad luck.

Straight Line, a journey, very pleasant.

Straight Lines are an indication of peace, happiness, and long life.

Swallow, a journey with a pleasant ending.

Swan, good luck and a happy marriage.

Sword, dispute, quarrels between lovers; a broken sword, victory of an enemy.

Timber, logs of timber indicate business success.

Toad, deceit and unexpected enemies.

Trees, a lucky sign; a sure indication of prosperity and happiness; surrounded by dots, a fortune in the country.

Triangles, always a sign of good luck and unexpected legacies.

Trident, success and honours in the Navy.

Twisted Figures, disturbances and vexation; grievances if there are many such figures.

Umbrella, annoyance and trouble.

Unicorn, scandal.

Vulture, bitter foes.

Wagon, a sign of approaching poverty.

Wavy Lines, if long and waved, denote losses and vexations. The importance of the lines depends upon the number of them and if heavy or light.

Wheel, an inheritance about to fall in.

Windmill, success in a venturous enterprise.

Wolf, beware of jealous intrigues.

Woman, pleasure and happiness; if accompanied by dots, wealth or children. Several women indicate scandal.

Wood, a speedy marriage.

Worms indicate secret foes.

Yacht, pleasure and happiness.

Yew-tree indicates the death of an aged person who will leave his possessions to the consultant.

Zebra, travel and adventure in foreign lands.

CHAPTER V

COLLECTION OF SPECIMEN CUPS, WITH INTERPRETATIONS

The succeeding ten figures are copied from actual tea-cups that have been at different times subjected to the proper ritual by various consultants and duly interpreted by seers. They are selected out of a larger number as being representative of many different classes of horoscope, and they should afford students practical instruction in what symbols to look for, and how to discern them clearly as they turn the cup about and about in their hands.

By reference to the interpretations provided upon the pages facing the illustrations he will be able to ascertain the principles upon which to form a judgment of the cup generally; and this, once he has mastered the method, he will be able to supplement, by consulting the alphabetical list of symbols and their significations in the previous chapter, and in this way will speedily attain proficiency in reading any tea-cup presented for his consideration.

INTERPRETATIONS AND ILLUSTRATIONS

INTERPRETATION
FIG. 1

This is a fortunate horoscope. If the cup has been turned by a man it shows that he will gain success, honour, and wealth in the profession of a naval officer. If by a woman then her luck is bound up with that of a sailor or marine.

The pistols on the sides show the profession of arms, and the naval gun in the bottom of the cup accompanied by a trident the branch to which he belongs. The pear on one side and the tree on the other are two of the best signs of promotion, rewards, and prosperity. The house near the pistol pointing towards the handle of the cup indicates the acquisition of property, but as neither tree nor house are surrounded by dots this will be a town, not a country, residence. The repetition of the initial 'L' may show the name of the admiral, ship, or battle in which the officer will win renown. The triangles confirm the other signs of good fortune.

FIG. 1

Principal Symbols

Two pistols on side.
A cannon in conjunction with a trident in centre.
A pear
A tree on sides.
A house.
A pair of compasses near the rim.
Several small triangles scattered about.
Initial letters 'L' (twice), 'N', and 'V' (twice).

INTERPRETATION

FIG. 2

There is nothing very significant in this tea-cup. The wavy lines denote a trouble-some journey leading to some small amount of luck in con-nection with a per son or place whose name begins with the initial 'E.' The hour-glass near the rim and the place from which the journey starts denotes that it will be undertaken in order to avoid some imminent peril. The numeral '4' conjoined with the sign of a parcel shows that one may be expected in that number of days.

FIG. 2

Principal Symbols

Wavy Lines.
Initial 'E' in conjunction with
Horse-shoe.
Hour-glass near rim.
Parcel in conjunction with numeral '4'.

INTERPRETATION

Fig. 3

This shows, by means of the crescent moon on the side, prosperity and fortune as the result of a journey denoted by the lines. The number of triangles in con junction with the initial 'H' indicates the receipt of a legacy from some person whose name commences with that letter, and, being near the rim, at no great distance of time. The bird flying towards and near the handle, accompanied by a triangle and a long envelope, denotes good news from an official source. The flag gives warning of some danger from an enemy.

FIG. 3

Principal Symbols

Crescent moon.
Bird flying.
Triangles.
Flag.
Initial 'A' in conjunction with sign of letter in official envelope.
Other initials, 'H' and two 'L's.

INTERPRETATION

FIG. 4

The consultant is about to journey east ward to some large building or institution, shown by the figure at the end of the straight line of dots. There is some con fusion in his or her affairs caused by too much indulgence in pleasure and gaiety, denoted by the butterfly involved in obscure groups of tea-leaves near the handle. The tree and the fleur-de-lys (or lily) in the bottom of the cup are, however, signs of eventual success, probably through the assistance of some person whose name be gins with an 'N.'

FIG. 4

Principal Symbols

Large tree in bottom of cup.
Fleur-de-lys (or lily).
Butterfly on side approaching handle.
Line of dots leading east to
Building.
Initials 'N' and 'C'.

INTERPRETATION

FIG. 5

A letter is approaching the consultant containing a considerable sum of money, as it is surrounded by dots. The future, shown by the bottom of the cup, is not clear, and betokens adversities; but the presence of the hammer there denotes triumph over these, a sign confirmed by the hat on the side. The consultant will be annoyed by somebody whose name begins with 'J,' and assisted by one bearing the initial 'Y.'

FIG. 5

Principal Symbols

Hammer in centre of bottom.
A letter approaching the house, accompanied by
Dots,
Hat,
Initials 'Y' and 'J' (accompanied by small cross).

INTERPRETATION

FIG. 6

A letter containing good news, shown by bird flying and the triangle, may be expected im-mediately. If from a lover it shows that he is constant and prosperous, owing to the anchor on the side. The large tree on the side indicates happiness and prosperity. A letter will be received from someone whose initial is 'L.' In the bottom of the cup there are signs of minor vexations or delays in connection with someone whose name begins with 'C.'

FIG. 6

Principal Symbols

Large tree on side.
Anchor on side.
Bird flying high towards handle.
Small cross in bottom.
Letter sign close to handle.
Triangle.
Initial 'I,' with letter sign.
Other initials, 'C' and 'H'.

INTERPRETATION

Fig. 7

The two horse-shoes indicate a lucky journey to some large residence in a north easterly direction, the tree surmounting which denotes that happiness and fortune will be found there and that (as it is surrounded by dots) it is situated in the country. The sitting hen in the bottom of the cup, surmounted by a triangle (to see which properly the illustration must be turned round) is indicative of increased wealth by an unexpected legacy. A letter from someone whose name begins with 'T' will contain a remittance of money, but it may not arrive for some little time.

FIG. 7

Principal Symbols

Large horse-shoe, edge of bottom, in conjunction with smaller horse-shoe.
Line of dots leading E.N.E. to
Large building surmounted by
Tree, overlapping rim.
Flowers.
Small triangles.
Initial 'T' with letter and money signs.

INTERPRETATION

FIG. 8

This tea-cup appears to give warning by the flag in conjunction with a rifle and the letter 'V' that some friend of the consult ant will be wounded in battle, and as there is a coffin in the bottom of the cup that the wounds will be fatal. On the other side, however, a sceptre, surrounded by signs of honours, seems to indicate that 'V' will be recognized by his sovereign and a decoration bestowed upon him for bravery in battle, shown by the initial 'K' accompanied by a letter-sign, and by the astrological sign of Mars, intervening between these and the sceptre.

FIG. 8

Principal Symbols

Coffin in bottom, in conjunction with 'V'.
Flag in conjunction with rifle on side.
Sceptre on side.
Large initial 'K' with letter sign near sceptre.
Astrological sign of Mars between them.
Initial 'V' near flag and rifle.

INTERPRETATION

FIG. 9

If the consultant be single this cup will, by means of the hare on the side, tell him that he will speedily be married. The figure of a lady holding out an ivy-leaf is a sign that his sweetheart will prove true and constant, and the heart in conjunction with a ring and the initial 'A' still further points to marriage with a person whose name begins with that letter. The flower triangle, and butterfly are all signs of prosperity , pleasure and happiness.

FIG. 9

Principal Symbol

Hare sitting on side.
Butterfly near rim.
Heart and ring.
Large flower on edge of bottom.
Figure of woman holding ivy-leaf in bottom.
Triangle.
Initials 'A' and 'C' with dots.

INTERPRETATION

FIG. 10

This is typical of the cup being too often consulted by some people. It is almost void of meaning, the only symbols indicating a short journey, although the flower near the rim denotes good luck, and the fact that the bottom is clear that nothing very important is about to happen to the consultant.

FIG. 10

Principal Symbols

Line of dots leading W.S.W. to Flower.

Two letters near rim.

CHAPTER VI

OMENS

How have omens been regarded in the past. An appeal to anciency is usually a safeguard for a basis. It is found that most of the earliest records are now subsisting. See official guide to the British Museum. Babylonian and Assyrian antiquities, table case H. Nineveh Gallery, the following appears:

"By means of omen tablets the Babylonian and Assyrian priests from time immemorial predicted events which they believed would happen in the near or in the remote future. They deduced these omens from the appearance and actions of animals, birds, fish, and reptiles; from the appearance of the entrails of sacrificial victims; from the appearance and condition of human and animal offspring at birth; from the state and condition of various members of the human body."

In India, where the records of the early ages of civilization go back hundreds of years, omens are considered of great importance. Later, in Greece, the home of the greatest and highest culture and civilization, we find, too, omens regarded very seriously, while today there are vast numbers of persons of intellect, the world over, who places reliance upon omens.

That there is some good ground for belief in some omens seems indisputable. Whether this has arisen as the result of experience, by the following of some particular event close upon the heels of signs observed, or whether it has been an intuitive science, in which provision has been used to afford an interpretation, is not quite clear. It seems idle to attempt to dismiss the whole thing as mere superstition, wild guessing, or abject credulity, as some try to do, with astrology and alchemy also, and other occult sciences; the fact remains that omens have, in numberless instances, given good warnings.

To say that these are just coincidences is to beg the question. For the universe is governed by law. Things happen because they must, not because they may. There is no such thing as ac-cident or coincidence. We may not be able to see the steps and the connections. But they are there all the same.

In years gone by many signs were deduced from the symptoms of sick men; the events or actions of a man's life; dreams and visions; the appearance of a man's shadow; from fire, flame, light, or smoke; the state and condition of cities and their streets, of fields, marshes, rivers, and lands. From the appearances of the stars and planets, of eclipses, meteors, shooting stars, the direction of winds, the form of clouds, thunder and lightning and other weather incidents, they were able to forecast happenings. A number of tablets are devoted to these prophecies.

It is conceivable that many of these omens should have found their way into Greece, and it is not unreasonable to believe that India may have derived her knowledge of omens from Babylonia; or it may have been the other way about. The greatest of scholars are divided in their opinions as to which really is the earlier civilization.

The point to be made here is that in all parts of the world—in quarters where we may be certain that no trace of Grecian, Indian, or Babylonian science or civilization has appeared—there are to be found systems of prophecies by omens.

It may be accounted for in two ways. One that in all races as they grow up, so to speak, there is the same course of evolution of ideas and superstition which to many appears childish. The other explanation seems to be the more reasonable one, if we believe, as we are forced to do, that omens do foretell—that all peoples, all races, accumulate a record, oral or other wise, of things which have happened more or less connected with things which seemed to indicate them. In course of time this knowledge appears to consolidate. It gets generally accepted as true. And then it is handed on from generation to generation. Often with the passage of years it gets twisted and a new meaning taken out of it altogether different from the original.

It would be difficult to attempt to classify omens. Many books have been written on the subject and more yet to be written of the beliefs of the various races. The best that can be offered here is a selection from one or other of the varied sources. In Greece sneezing was a good omen and was considered a proof of the truth of what was said at the moment by the sneezer.

A tingling in the hand denoted the near handling of money, a ringing in the ears that news will soon be received. The number of sneezes then became a sign for more definite results. The hand which tingled, either right or left, indicated whether it were to be paid or received. The particular ear affected was held to indicate good or evil news. Other involuntary movements of the body were also considered of prime importance.

Many omens are derived from the observation of various substances dropped into a bowl of water. In Babylon oil was used. Today in various countries melted lead, wax, or the white of an egg, is used. From the shapes which result, the trade or occupation of a future husband, the luck for the year, and so on, are deduced in the folk practices of modern Europe. Finns use stearine and melted lead, Magyars lead, Russians wax, Danes lead and egg, and the northern counties of England egg, wax and oil.

Bird omens were the subject of very serious study in Greece. It has been thought that this was because in the early mythology of Greece some of their gods and goddesses were believed to have been birds. Birds, therefore, were particularly sacred, and their appearances and movements were of profound significance. The principal birds for signs were the raven, the crow, the heron, wren, dove, woodpecker, and kingfisher, and all the birds of prey, such as the hawk, eagle, or vulture, which the ancients classed together (W. R. Halliday, *Greek Divination*). Many curious instances, which were fulfilled, of bird omens are related in *The Other World* by Rev. F. Lee. A number of families have traditions about the appearance of a white bird in particular.

"In the ancient family of Ferrers, of Chartley Park, in Staffordshire, a herd of wild cattle is preserved. A tradition arose in the time of Henry III that the birth of a parti-coloured calf is a sure omen of death, within the same year, to a member of the Lord Ferrers family. By a noticeable coincidence, a calf of this description has been born whenever a death has happened of late years in this noble family." (Staffordshire Chronicle, July, 1835). The falling of a picture or a statue or bust of the individual is usually regarded as an evil omen. Many cases are cited where this has been soon followed by the death of the person.

It would be easy to multiply instances of this sort of personal omen or warning. The history and traditions of our great families are saturated with it. The predictions and omens relating to certain well known families, and others, recur at once; and from these it may be inferred that beneath the more popular beliefs there is enough fire and truth to justify the smoke that is produced, and to reward some of the faith that is placed in the modern dreambooks and the books of fate and the interpretations of omens.

Omens

Acorn—Falling from the oak tree on anyone, is a sign of good fortune to the person it strikes.

Bat—To see one in day time means long journey.

Birthdays—

"Monday's child is fair of face,
Tuesday's child is full of grace,
Wednesday's child is full of woe,
Thursday's child has far to go,
Friday's child is loving and giving,
Saturday's child works hard for its living;
But a child that's born on the Sabbath day
Is handsome and wise and loving and gay."

Butterfly—In your room means great pleasure and success, but you must not catch it, or the luck will change.

Candle—A spark on the wick of a candle means a letter for the one who first sees it. A big glow like a parcel means money coming to you.

Cat—Black cat to come to your house

means difficulties caused by treachery. Drive it away and avoid trouble.

Chain—If your chain breaks while on you means disappointments or a broken engagement of marriage.

Clothes To put on clothes. the wrong way out is a sign of good luck; but you must not alter them, or the luck will change.

Clover—To find a four-leaf clover means luck to you, happiness and prosperity.

Cow—Coming in your yard or garden a very prosperous sign.

Crickets—A lucky omen. It foretells money coming to you. They should not be disturbed.

Dog—Coming to your house, means faithful friends and a favourable sign.

Death-Watch—A clicking in the wall by this little insect is regarded as evil, but it does not necessarily mean a death; possibly only some sickness.

Ears—You are being talked about if your ear tingles. Some say, "right for spite, left for love." Others reverse this omen. If you think of the person, friend, or acquaintance who is likely to be talking of you, and mention the name aloud, the tingling will cease if you say the right one.

Flag—If it falls from the staff, while flying it means danger from wounds inflicted by an enemy.

Fruit Stones or Pips—Think of a wish first, and then count your stones or pips. If the number is even, the omen is good. If odd, the reverse is the case.

Grasshopper in the house means some great friend or distinguished person will visit you.

Horseshoe—To find one means it will bring you luck.

Knives grossed are a bad omen. If a knife or fork or scissors falls to the ground and sticks in the floor you will have a visitor.

Ladybirds betoken visitors.

Looking Glass—To break means it will bring you ill luck.

Magpies—One, bad luck; two, good luck; three, a wedding; four, a birth.

Marriage—A maid should not wear colours; a widow never white. happy omens for brides are sunshine and a cat sneezing.

May—"Marry in May, and you'll rue the day."

New Moon on a Monday signifies good luck

and good weather. The new moon seen for the first time over the right shoulder offers the chance for a wish to come true.

NIGHTINGALE—Lucky for lovers if heard before the cuckoo.

OWLS are evil omens. Continuous hooting of owls in your trees is said to be one of ill-health.

PIGS—To meet a sow coming towards you is good; but if she turns away, the luck flies.

RABBITS—A rabbit running across your path is said to be unlucky.

RAT—A rat running in front of you means treacherous servants and losses through enemies.

RAVEN—To see one, means death to the aged or trouble generally.

SALT spilled means a quarrel. This may be avoided by throwing a pinch over the left shoulder.

SCISSORS—If they fall and stick in the floor it means quarrels, illness, separation of lovers.

SERPENT OR SNAKE—If it crosses your path, means spiteful enemies, bad luck. Kill it and your luck will be reversed.

SHOES—The right shoe is the best one to put on first.

Shooting Stars—If you wish, while the star is still moving, your wish will come true.

Singing before breakfast, you'll cry before night.

Spiders—The little red spider is the money spider, and means good fortune coming to you. It must not be disturbed. Long-legged spiders are also forerunners of good fortune.

Towel—To wipe your hands on a towel at the same time with another, means you are to quarrel with him or her in the near future.

Wheel—The wheel coming off any vehicle you are riding in means you are to inherit some fortune, a good omen.

Washing Hands—If you wash your hands in the water just used by another, a quarrel may be expected, unless you first make the sign of the cross over the water.

1993 Addendum:

And don't forget the imaginary ha-ha, a bird of good omen in China.

J.N.P

AFTERWORD

by
John Harney

People have been drinking tea for about 5,000 years. It's a safe guess that's about how long they've been reading tea leaves as well. This book on the subject had lain forgotten perhaps half a century in the musty old book dealer's shop where I found it. Only after I mentioned it in the course of a presentation about tea did I come to realize how interested we all seem to remain in what tea leaves have to say: I received more questions about reading the leaves than about anything else. This happened in one presentation after another. Requests to borrow this irreplaceable book have become so frequent that I decided to reprint it, if only out of self-defense.

The first person with whom I discussed the idea was James Norwood Pratt, author of the beloved classic *The Tea Lover's Treasury*. My noted tea-writer friend turned out to be a leaf reader as well. I wanted to know what to make of the whole thing; is there anything to it? "If your book is any good, I'll write an introduction to it and I'll tell you." Well, my book turns out to be the earliest on the subject anybody has ever found and teaches an authentic tradition which goes back centuries in Britain. I was pleased he found it a good book and feel it is even better with an introduction by James Norwood Pratt. I think the most intriguing statement he makes is "there is nothing 'mere' about coincidence—the universe is *nothing but* coincidence." Is this the secret of The Tea Leaf Oracle? I still don't know what to make of reading tea leaves actually, except to say it's obviously fun, costs no money, and any group of six or eight is likely to include som one with above average talent for it.

I don't need tea leaves to tell me that those who use the Genuine Article receive infinitely more pleasure than the teabag dunkers among us. When my passion for fine teas got me into the business years ago, it was never my ambition to rival the mass-market supermarket brands. John Harney & Sons teas are intended exclusively for the individual who realizes pleasure is far too serious to take lightly. They must be handled respectfully and brewed properly, never less than three full minutes and in many cases longer. We offer no instant gratification, just abiding pleasure.

Serious pleasure seekers will eventually discover the various delights of robust black teas for breakfast, mellow midday oolongs, tasty even when the pot's cold, the up-lift of great Darjeelings as afternoon tea, or the solace of a quiet green at night. They might also discover that Harney & Sons teas are hard to beat. Bragging is cheaper than advertising, but I won't go on and on. I'll just say I predict great enjoyment for any reader of tea leaves who discovers our fine teas. Ask for our catalog and seek the perfect thing to suit every individual mood.